NOTE

100 Tunes to Play is a series of ten books, each consisting of ten easy arrangements for instrument and piano of music by a famous composer (see back cover).

Three instrumental parts, identical apart from pitch and clef, are inserted in each piano score:

Treble Clef in C (suitable for recorder, flute, oboe, and violin)

Treble Clef in B flat (suitable for clarinet and trumpet)

Bass clef (suitable for cello and bassoon)

CONTENTS

Book 9 (Tchaikovsky)

1. WALTZ
(from Swan Lake Op.20)

Printed in Great Britain

OXFORD UNIVERSITY PRESS, MUSIC DEPARTMENT, WALTON STREET, OXFORD OX2 6DP

2. CHANSON TRISTE
(Op.40 No.2)

Allegro non troppo

* Lower notes should be played when accompanying cello or bassoon.

3. MARCH

(from The Nutcracker Suite Op.71a)

Tempo di marcia viva

✱ Lower notes should be played when accompanying cello or bassoon.

TUNES TO PLAY

Arranged by
Kenneth Pont

Book 9
TCHAIKOVSKY

Treble Clef in B flat

OXFORD UNIVERSITY PRESS

1. WALTZ
(from Swan Lake Op.20)

Treble Clef in B♭

2. CHANSON TRISTE
(Op.40 No.2)

Printed in Great Britain

OXFORD UNIVERSITY PRESS, MUSIC DEPARTMENT, WALTON STREET, OXFORD OX2 6DP

3. MARCH
(from The Nutcracker Suite Op.71a)

4. ANDANTE CANTABILE
(from String Quartet in D Op.11)

5. DANSE RUSSE TREPAK

(from The Nutcracker Suite Op.71a)

6. WALTZ

(from Symphony No.5 in E minor Op.64)

7. THEME

(from Piano Concerto in B♭ minor Op.23)

8. ALLEGRO MOLTO VIVACE
(from Symphony No.6 in B minor Op.74)

8

9. A LEGEND
(from Chansons pour la Jeunesse Op.54 No.5)

10. WALTZ
(from The Sleeping Beauty Op.66)

TUNES TO PLAY

Arranged by
Kenneth Pont

Book 9
TCHAIKOVSKY

Treble Clef in C

OXFORD UNIVERSITY PRESS

1. WALTZ

(from Swan Lake Op.20)

2. CHANSON TRISTE

(Op.40 No.2)

Printed in Great Britain

OXFORD UNIVERSITY PRESS, MUSIC DEPARTMENT, WALTON STREET, OXFORD OX2 6DP

3. MARCH

(from The Nutcracker Suite Op.71a)

4. ANDANTE CANTABILE

(from String Quartet in D Op.11)

5. DANSE RUSSE TREPAK

(from The Nutcracker Suite Op.71a)

6. WALTZ
(from Symphony No.5 in E minor Op.64)

7. THEME
(from Piano Concerto in B♭ minor Op.23)

8. ALLEGRO MOLTO VIVACE
(from Symphony No.6 in B minor Op.74)

9. A LEGEND
(from Chansons pour la Jeunesse Op.54 No.5)

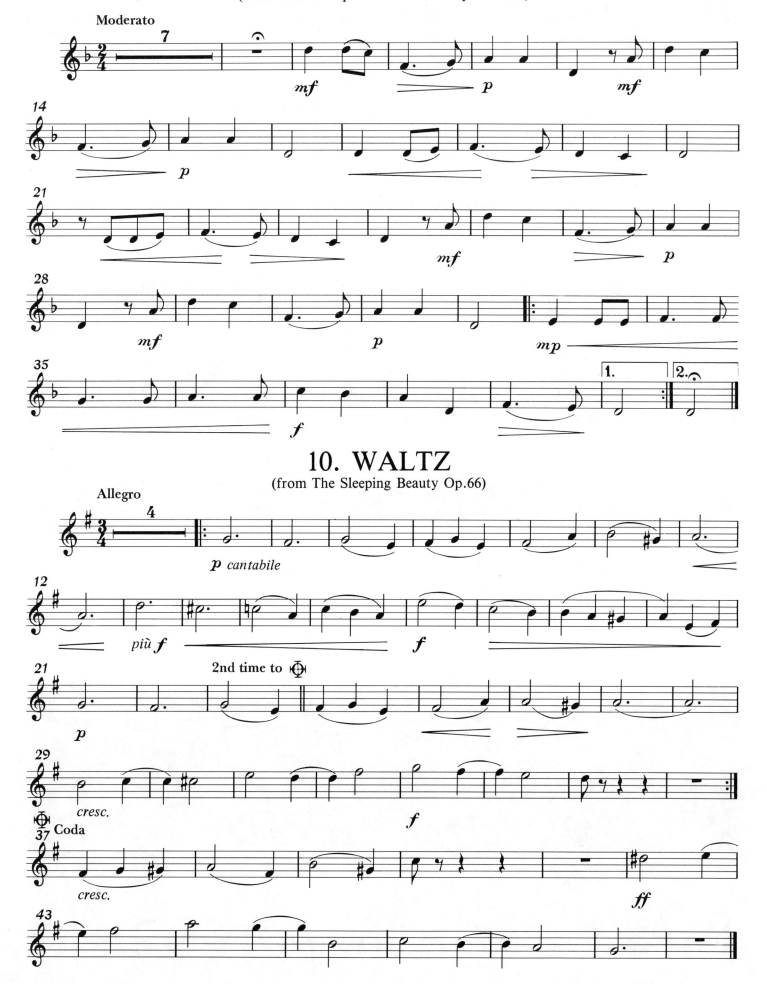

10. WALTZ
(from The Sleeping Beauty Op.66)

TUNES TO PLAY

Arranged by
Kenneth Pont

Book 9
TCHAIKOVSKY

Bass Clef

OXFORD UNIVERSITY PRESS

1. WALTZ
(from Swan Lake Op.20)

Bass Clef

2. CHANSON TRISTE
(Op.40 No.2)

3. MARCH
(from The Nutcracker Suite Op.71a)

Tempo di marcia viva

4

4. ANDANTE CANTABILE
(from String Quartet in D Op.11)

5. DANSE RUSSE TREPAK

(from The Nutcracker Suite Op.71a)

6. WALTZ
(from Symphony No.5 in E minor Op.64)

7. THEME
(from Piano Concerto in B♭ minor Op.23)

8. ALLEGRO MOLTO VIVACE
(from Symphony No.6 in B minor Op.74)

8

9. A LEGEND
(from Chansons pour la Jeunesse Op.54 No.5)

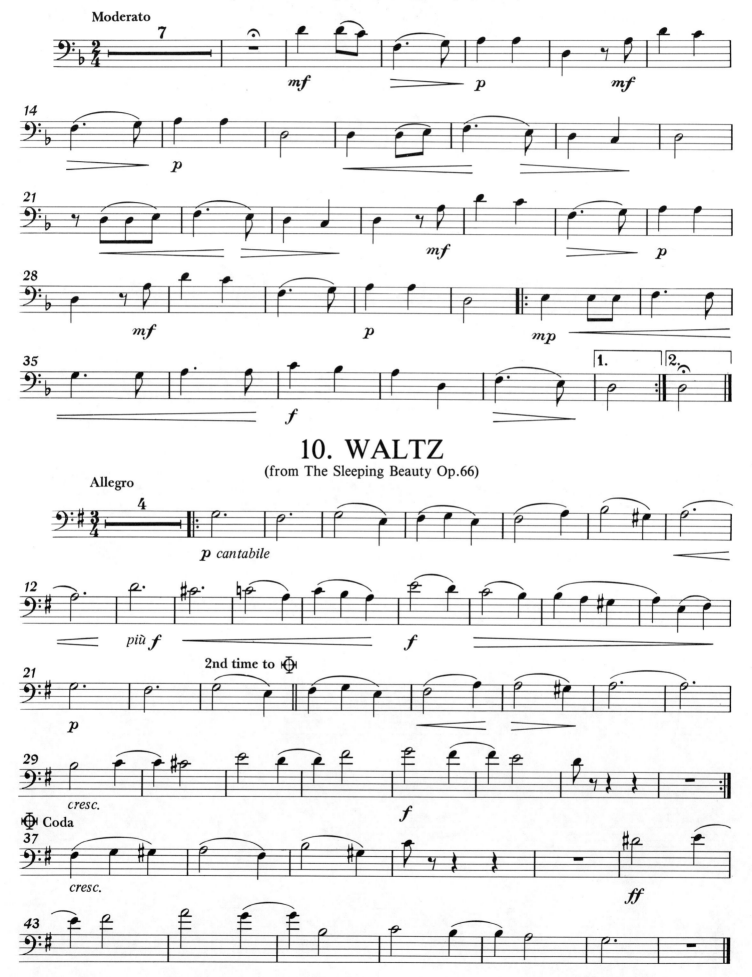

10. WALTZ
(from The Sleeping Beauty Op.66)

* Lower notes should be played when accompanying cello or bassoon.

4. ANDANTE CANTABILE
(from String Quartet in D Op.11)

Andante cantabile

2nd time to ⊕

* Play LH throughout an octave lower (except where marked loco) when accompanying cello or bassoon.

5. DANSE RUSSE TREPAK

(from The Nutcracker Suite Op.71a)

* This passage should be played an octave lower when accompanying cello or bassoon.

6. WALTZ
(from Symphony No.5 in E minor Op.64)

* octaves only necessary when accompanying cello or bassoon.

7. THEME
(from Piano Concerto in B♭ minor Op.23)

Andante non troppo e molto maestoso

8. ALLEGRO MOLTO VIVACE
(from Symphony No.6 in B minor Op.74)

* This passage to be played an octave lower when accompanying cello or bassoon.

9. A LEGEND

(from Chansons pour la Jeunesse Op.54 No.5)

Moderato

* Lower notes should be played when accompanying cello or bassoon.

10. WALTZ
(from The Sleeping Beauty Op.66)